Also by Alan Riach

Poetry

This Folding Map
An Open Return
First & Last Songs
From the Vision of Hell: An Extract of Dante

Criticism

Hugh MacDiarmid's Epic Poetry
The Poetry of Hugh MacDiarmid

Clearances

Alan Riach

Publication of this book has been assisted by a publishing grant from Creative New Zealand.

Copyright © 2001 Alan Riach
First published 2001

The author asserts his moral rights in the work.

This book is copyright. Except for the purposes of fair reviewing, no part of this publication may be reproduced or transmitted in any form or by any means, electronic or mechanical, including photocopying, recording, or any information storage and retrieval system, including the internet and the World Wide Web, without permission in writing from the publisher.
Infringers of copyright render themselves liable to prosecution.

ISBN 1-877270-07-5

Published by Hazard Press Limited
and Scottish Cultural Press

Hazard Press Ltd
P.O. Box 2151, Christchurch, New Zealand
email: info@hazard.co.nz
www.hazard.co.nz

Scottish Cultural Press
Unit 13d, Newbattle Road, Dalkeith, EH22 3LJ, Scotland
email: info@scottishbooks.com
www.scottishbooks.com

Cover illustration: 'Shoreline, Ardnamurchan' by John Cunningham
Author photo courtesy of Campus Photography, University of Waikato
Printed in Christchurch, New Zealand

Acknowledgements

Some of the poems collected here, or earlier versions of them, have been published in the following journals: in New Zealand, in *Landfall, Sport, The Listener, Poetry New Zealand, SPAN* and the *Waikato Journal of Education*; in Scotland, in *Chapman, Lines Review, Poetry Scotland* and *The New Shetlander*; and in *PN Review* (Manchester), *Southfields* (London), *The Literary Review* (USA), *The Literary Quarterly* (India), *Island* (Tasmania) and *Quadrant* (Australia). Some have been broadcast on Radio New Zealand Concert FM, the National Programme, UFM (Waikato) and BBC Radio Scotland.

Poems have also appeared in the following books: *Back to the Light: New Glasgow Poems*, edited by Donny O'Rourke and Hamish Whyte (Glasgow: Mariscat Press, 2001); *New Zealand Love Poems: An Oxford Anthology*, edited by Lauris Edmond (Auckland: Oxford University Press, 2000); *Jewels in the Water: New Zealand Poetry for Younger Readers*, edited by Terry Locke (Hamilton, NZ: Leaders Press/University of Waikato, 2000); *Doors: A Contemporary New Zealand Poetry Selection*, edited by Terry Locke (Hamilton, NZ: Leaders Press/University of Waikato, 2000); *Unknown Is Best: A Celebration of Edwin Morgan at Eighty*, edited by Robyn Marsack and Hamish Whyte (Glasgow & Edinburgh: Mariscat Press & Scottish Poetry Library, 27 April 2000), *Love for Love: An Anthology of Love Poems*, edited by John Burnside and Alec Finlay (Edinburgh: Morning Star Publications/ Polygon, 2000); 'Port of Auckland' and 'Spar Cave, Isle of Skye' were commissioned and selected by the National Museum of Scotland for an exhibition of poster-poems (on display 1999-2000) and published in the anthology *Scotland to the World to Scotland: Poems of Arrival and Departure (Present Poets 2)*, compiled by Jenni Calder (Edinburgh: NMS Publishing, 1999); *César Vallejo: Translations, Transformations, Tributes*, edited by Richard Price and Stephen Watts (London and Oxford: Southfields Press/Au Quai Editions, 1998); *Carmichael's Book: A Homage to Alexander Carmichael's Carmina Gadelica*, edited by Alec Finlay (Edinburgh: Morning Star/Inverness: Artbook, 1998); *Below the Surface: Words and Images in Protest at French Testing on Moruroa*, edited by Aubrey Hall (Auckland: Vintage New Zealand/ Random House, 1995); *Contraflow on the Super Highway*, edited by W.N. Herbert and Richard Price (London: Southfields Press/Gairfish, 1994). I am grateful to the editors of these books and periodicals, and to John Dixon, David Foreman, Bill Manhire, John Purser, Kevin Ireland, Les Murray, Marshall Walker and Edwin Morgan. 'We must never give in to the angels.'

Quotations in 'The Coral Island' are taken from the *Agricola* of Tacitus and 'Another Epitaph on an Army of Mercenaries' by Hugh MacDiarmid; the epigraph is from Walter Benjamin, 'Theses on the Philosophy of History' (part VI). The quotation in 'Spar Cave, Isle of Skye' is from Charles Olson, *The Maximus Poems* (section IV) and the last two lines allude to Edwin Morgan's 'The Summons' from his *Sonnets from Scotland*. The epigraph to the opening section is stolen from Richard Stark's novel *Comeback*. He attributes it to a Chinese Fortune Cookie.

Contents

1. *Capstan Bars*

Drinan	10
Traces of Ain	11
Port of Auckland	12
Spar Cave, Isle of Skye	13
Wellington Harbour	14
The Studio: Air	15

2. *Storm Warnings*

The Flood	17
The Coral Island	18
Antenor	20
The Wall	21
The State	23
Lamento	24
The Resistable Rise	26
The Castle	27
The Knight	29
December	30
The Place of Lost Roads	31
The Burning Deck	32

3. *Clearances*

Kilmartin Glen	34
The Rivers of Space	35
A Proper Respect for Horses	36
Edinburgh, High Street: Nocturne	38
Cities on the Plain	40
Insomnia 3	41
Nostalgia	42
New Zealand Pastoral	44
Clearances	45

Kylesku	47
Going Away Poem	48
Paint	49
Cézanne	50
Passacaglia	51
Sankey Hymns	53
MacDiarmid on Whalsay	54
The Jungle Books	56
The Symphony of a Thousand	58
The Viaduct, Millheugh	60

4. *The Long Reach*

To My Brother	62
Trilce 61	63
Lullaby	65
Kissing in Cars	66
The Long Reach	67
Of Love	68
The Transit of Venus	69
Late Afternoon	70

1

Capstan Bars

The outcome you have waited for is assured.
Continue to persevere.

Drinan
for John Purser

New room, after new room: sunlight
on the stairwell, pine banisters
and landing, behind a wall of books a secret doorway,
music, a hundred thousand patterns of
a history of tragedies, of laughter, and
of beauty in the places that the earth makes
here for us (we take and only add, sometimes,
a very small amount). It must have been
a lucky day, when accidental words or just
a glance might lead to recognition, and
the pattern might begin to open out, effortlessly,
like something unravelling, yet fought for,
as salmon do, rock pool between torrents, to one other
new room, flashing suspended in sunlight, space,
between the bright banisters, river and air,
where every room is sunlight, telling you to stay,
and every act is building
to put your flesh to use a better way.

Traces of Ain

*The Gaelic for whisky means water of life. The Navaho
have several words; one is Todilhil, water of darkness.*

The Firth of Thames is Caribbean blue.
Darkness moves the currents under bright creole.

The trace in your voice is a slanting light
that comes from a long spent star. You can't recall

its name but it informs us. Stop the car, get out by Whalebone Stream,
breathe salt air and listen to the tide, stretching.

Port of Auckland

New Zealand Herald, 9.12.98: Shipping News
From Sydney, 12.45pm: *Botany Bay*

Too far away, the ship swings in: my father's eyes
clock funnel, colours, movement, recognise *Bayline*
I listen to his pilot's voice quietly speak Scots:
I stood upon that bridge, along the London River
some other morning now too old to detail, but
close enough to know. The sun and stars and moon
make charts and keep us moving. On Orakei Jetty by
Bastion Rock, a spit reaching out from the near,
that seems as though it might go on forever into
blatant sky, we pause before we back along, and
watch her slowly clear. My young son takes my hand
suddenly scared, the wind he walks into will rise.

Spar Cave, Isle of Skye

The pull beneath the water running over stone
revokes you, thresholds, links this living body
to inorganic pasts. 'The original unit survives
in the salt' breeze blowing now a world away,
within Spar Cave. I wish it could be clear, as easily
as I lean down, push my hand down, through sheets
of running water, grip the quilted limestone, see
the water up to my wrist, a bangle of ice: solid,
petrified flesh, frozen desire, primal alteration
in the zones that lie inside us and the cave there
in the stone. So our love keeps, travels with us?
I'll carry it forever. I speak with your voice.

Wellington Harbour

You're half-asleep. Outside, the streetlights glow,
the air comes gently southwards, through the open window,
the hillside houses, slanted roof, the pelmet slightly skew,
the cluttered gardens, toys and books: it hardly worries you.
Sleep slowly lifts our quiet bed, as magic carpets do.
Meanings turn to fancies, Christmas to New
Year, and this December season's residue.
Then a dream from faraway: a book you thought you knew,
opens on your own name, staring back at you.
And a voice breathes out: *let go, let go, close the book, be true* –
in the yellow lighted air come through the window, then, *hold on* –
this soft summer night in Wellington.

The Studio: Air

Perhaps an unremarked inhabitation is
what raises you from depths, as if
an ambience of oil and paint and canvas
frames and easels, brushes, that marble palette
table-top, the richest sworls of colour
on it, the rags with which to clean:
so much of it could speak of strength and certainty
so much is bright potential, the possible scene.
Here's a place where balance is the nurtured
thing, the possible dance perpetual. Wall
to wall, a warmth, a high adventure,
all through life, the most important things
are deemed the matter, and to ourselves
who know, will need no further speaking of.

2

Storm Warnings

The Flood

The rain came down past Saturation Point.
The tidal river burst its banks and water ran out, sweeping
down upon the houses on this side, flooded
the far-off marshes, over there. Tonight,

by moonlight, from the upstairs bedroom window, you can see
the flooded fields, as pale as milk and thinned in distance;
the river disappeared, its line or band submerged in
its own ocean; spread clusters of tiled roofs, obliques,

the steeply angled roof and high straight spire of church
rising like islands and causeways, over the teeming tide.
But here below the window, the great grey waves crash down
and the wind blows up and over, raising the waves through

fences, into our back garden, half-way up:
a surge of water volumes into weight, and joins the storming gale
to tear up that old apple tree I climbed on as a boy; it
rips it out and floats it helpless up towards the washing line's

flagpole, pushing it to lean, its timber creaks like a mast in a storm,
then our neighbours' fence gives way and walls of water
fall across the rising flood as angled current charging
over tended garden drowns it now forever as it goes —

The Coral Island

Even the dead will not be safe from this enemy,
if he wins.

The border was there. We had been protected.
Today the shield is broken. Nothing but waves, and
      rocks,
and Empire's bleak intentions to englut: an ocean
breaking past us, on our sense of what should be.
      Justice
is for everyone, and anyone to see; but judgement now is
      singular, and
all last things are lonely.

The ocean that surrounds our isolation
                    is unpredicted element.
We trust to its encircling and resounding;
we are committed to it,
      in the end.

The fleet is our example: set sail, set
          keel to current cross-wise
              with wreckage to fear, brave hearted,
women and men with knowledge of
          the consequence most likely:
Casualties of war, the wrong end of empire,
          stupidity of suits, the fluency of lies.
A struggle that always continues, in words and in
      these human lives.

This, not Ralph nor Peterkin, prevails
day after day, night after night, calling out for freedom from
the wrong that is as one with empire's name.

These people are pledged:
their grasp is all the world, and they are strange,
for they will attack the poor as violently as the rich.
'Theft, destruction, rape, these liars name Empire.

They make a desert, and they call it peace.'

In spite of their kind, 'some elements of worth
With difficulty persist, here and there on the earth.'

Antenor
(after A.P. Rossiter, on *Troilus and Cressida*)
for Marshall

When I was told once, long ago, to write an essay on
'The character in Shakespeare you'd most like to talk to'
I'd never heard of Antenor. Now, he'd be my man. Perhaps
you haven't noticed him? Never mind. You will,
next time you read the play. Five times he enters, maybe six.
And five times he goes out, as silent as he came.
He never speaks a line. He never utters a word.
And when the others talk of him, they talk as if he isn't there
and he doesn't object.

I see him in a dark prophetic outline:
the profile of a good man caught in war.
He didn't choose the world he's in,
and can't get out or reach beyond its limits.
Nor is he scandalized. No protest would be adequate, he knows.
He simply will not use his voice
when speech is so corrupted.
He is a strong and silent man.
Shakespeare's only one.

The Wall

— We arrived in Munich at 7 am, and
spent the day at the Bierfest, at long wooden tables:
Steins of lager, roasted half-chickens,
platters of wurst and cheeses; rubicund men in stockings
and bibbed shorts, and little hats with pheasant feathers,
dancing in formation on the raised square roped-off stages.
Their eyes were all shine, from alcohol and exertion,
but it looked as though they were thinking of something else
going on elsewhere, even as they lifted their knees
and slapped the sides of their shorts
to the brassy blare and tinkling of the music.

Perhaps it was simply that we had grown up
in the 60s, on films like *The Quiller Memorandum*, perhaps
it was also that we had read Brecht and Döblin and Ödön von Horváth's
Tales from the Vienna Woods, but all the merriment gave us the sense
that something else was going on elsewhere.

The next day, we went to the galleries: Raphael and Rembrandt,
Kandinsky and Franz Marc: *Deer in Snow*.
Blue Horses. Panthers, tigers, giant shores.

That evening we were walking back when we heard the sirens.

At exactly half past eleven that night, a man had exploded a bomb
at the gateway to the Bierfest, killing himself and half a dozen others
in the blast. Photojournals, later that day,
carried lurid pictures of the corpses scattered on the ground:
twenty-four hours, to the minute, to the spot,
we'd been there on the day before, walking out.

The wall can come down as easily as that. A seed can catch.
A play of light through the membrane —
A breaking of dawn through the porthole of a plane —

— Savour the moment; it is all now
a new configuration. Yet still I have this sense

of something else that's going on in other places, other than
the seen. Multi-story carparks in the West at 1 am
are instant Berlin. I boarded the plane in Auckland,
came down in London, and the Wall had come down.
It wasn't the Europe I'd left. I felt a strange nostalgia.
Once, if you'd had wings, you could have stood upon the Brandenburg
and looked both ways with your imagination. Now,
the armies of civilians, their children and their babies,
are mingling in the days and nights,
and saints and gargoyles wander with
the angels in the crowds.

The State

It doesn't matter where
you are: a Mexican
stand-off in Belfast, the eyes
on the back of your neck as you're walking
the corridor, an iron wall
come down like a sheet,
invisible, between the architrave and hall.
The FBI investigate
the bombed plane, mid-air,
230 passengers and wreckage
in the desolate Atlantic: these
moments live in your imagination
because of it, because you're
there: taking the walk
to the chair, cuffs and ankles
open for the straps. For others,
it's the look on your face, or maybe just cheap
comedy; for you, it's the set of your mind
that shapes it. What
in God's name keeps you steady,
walking? What,
but gravity and
forward motion,
all matter moves
to what end: unknowable, foreknown?

Lamento

He was bred into exile, learnèd in
elaboration (bluntness being
too easy 'at home'). He took
the risks like a good
diplomat, living and working
hard, without a passport.

When he talked of his country,
he remembered it as it really was:
a quality of absence —
parentheses that closed
before they opened —
brackets, back to back —
So it had been, for generations gone.

So better to say he was bred
for exile, thriving
upon it, mastering abroad
the lost skills and cunning he
had never had at home. (Home

is a deal made with midnight,
— an unpaid debt,
— an uncrossed book,
— a haunting, after all,
— a love betrayed by others, or
one other, as well as yourself.)

— Now he welcomes
foreigners, acquires the trick
of speaking like them, quickly, but
keeps his voice,
watches their ugly hands applauding,
negotiates, keeps mum, suspects.
He's recognised
removal from the only home
he knows now, and

asks himself in silence, with this
sheer determination,
what has he learned? What will he learn?
What will he turn his learning to?
And what will home become?

The Resistable Rise

How easily the symptoms show, Arturo!
How quickly it comes, unopposed
(Or opposition put aside by officers).
Arturo, tell me: Did you know
how readily your victory would clear
the crest of the tidal horizon?
The little god who raised you to your chair
must have seen a thing in you he liked.
But there are other gods, and wiser.
Wisdom doesn't always lack in power
and tides have a habit of turning;
but still the speed of the thing
impresses: how silently the others let it
happen, how comic it all appears
from the outside, how hateful it
actually is. A microcosm, then:
how any group of people might allow to prosper
the regime of the monstrous and maniacal.
Such as yourself, Arturo, Artura:
Such as yourself and your minions.

The Castle

an emptiness you could call emptiness provided you called vacant and empty the silent and lifeless terrain in front of a mobilized army or peaceful the vestibule to a powder magazine or quiet the spillway under the locks of a dam — a sense not of waiting but of incrementation
— Faulkner

I
The first thing to fall is silence. Imagination's leprosy.
The poisoned air is empty, then, of all you'd find conducive to —
No. Just empty, but with pressure in it, pressing
back and out: *Keep away, keep away. I'm dangerous. I am in charge.*
While also, *Now, attend! Be here! Be bowed, beneath me.*
Kafka's corridors: shafts without warmth, without sense.
Bach echoes tinnily, thin from some cheap portable, echoes hit
and spin from wall to wall, a savage claim on civil reason:
This air has no listening in it. All those empty spaces.
Mandelstam's silences. Perpetual threat. A Belfast opposition.
Ocivity. Language at its most banal. Pettiness accumulates
clichés of the sheer inane. You're in it now. Go on.

II
This domain is regal, monstrous, viciously guarded, evil:
No conversation happens for there's no-one there to talk to.
No change will seem possible and time does not inure but just
effects deterioration. Did Stalin sit complete as this, with a minor blunt
official there nearby, to bully? To threaten with complicity, bring into line,
helping to administer a general death to others? Everything gets ragged.
It atomises, parsimony, crushing as it separates, emmet-like
the minions, but crazed with competition. The art of collective sniggering
excels itself. Passion is in resentment only. Conviction only in greed.
She looks and says unspoken words: 'Don't talk to me about these things:
Only I shall tell you what the truth is. You will listen. Never smile.
(I will not learn. I cannot learn. I will not recognise you further.)'

III
Reluctantly, K.'s feet go up the stairs — or down them,
carrying beyond the flesh the spirit to a world of evident wrong,

Sisyphus daily. Kafka nods impatiently. 'Poetry's
a mug's game. You're not here for that. You're here to suffer
what you know now once was done and can't be done again.'
And the creature in the office there presiding over Belsen
takes medals from the officers of Cowardice. The rictus grin. Correctness in
a world where Osrics thrive. Roderigo's gulled. Iago sneers, successfully,
'Put money in thy purse.' 'Ah yes,' says Kafka, now tight-lipped. 'But
how else would you have it? This is the creature's victory, the era of
eclipse. There is no court of higher appeal. You say you believe
in a world of actual value. This is its deepest measure. Keep it in mind.'

The Knight

You want to know what it's like, being a knight?
Fucking terrible. First you wake up before dawn, listening for birds.
You hear the birds singing but you don't want to hear
the birds singing because that's sleep fucked.

And you have to get up and get into the armour.
It's fucking enormous, and heavy, really heavy.
Bit by bit, breastplate, gauntlets, visored helmet,
so heavy you can't walk. You don't have style. It isn't cool.

Have you ever thought how tight it gets
when you're winched up by your joints and your crutch
and lifted over above this fucking great horse
that runs like an engine when it runs which isn't

often but it will today, because today's all
jousting, and if you can keep the heavy, heavy lance
steady in your hand as you're galloping along
fast as your armour will let you, you're dreaming of a

simple twist of the forearm and wrist that'll take
the point of the lance into an angle
not suspected, because that's just what you're
supposed to do, being a knight? And if you get through the day,

the whole day, like this, one fucking joust after another,
you've still got to spend fucking hours
at night, taking all this clobber off, before
you get to go to bed, scared of waking up

next morning. And you lie there weary, tired down
to the marrow, and you can't sleep anyway
at all that well. And you don't dream.
And you're very tired and heavy in the morning.

That's what it's like. Being a knight. Fuck it.

December

I'm sitting with my back to London, travelling south by train,
leaving Scotland to cold disappointments & snow
clouds boiling up in the drab rolling borders, hills
lost in sperm-grey mist, rivers
half-frozen (their water would taste
of iron & sheep)
sheep, like pellets, like blanched rabbit droppings,
garlic pearls
fishfood
yellowed as jaundice with distance in valleys
of dolls'
houses
    — a thick black burst of crows
scatters the horizon
soot & charcoal shreds
last year's letters to Santa
as if to say with Van Gogh quickness, Bang!
— straight out the shotgun of winter.

The Place of Lost Roads

Over the lawn in the garden, up on the slope where the
bushes are and the cabbage trees, there's a square
translucent space. This is the place of lost roads. I know
what it is. I tell myself, looking through the sliding
glass doors of the living room, the blinds drawn up, that
it's just the reflection of the rectangular kitchen window,
refracted through the living room doors, and now, from
where I sit, projected: an oblong square translucent space,
a plane with four sides, an open door that penetrates or
cuts through all the bushes, trees and plants that grow there.

It's easy to explain it like that.

That isn't what it is.

It's opening a newspaper and finding a name —
a name you believed you'd forgotten —
someone you loved once you thought who had died.

This is the place of lost roads.

The Burning Deck

The window of my bedroom overlooked the roofs:
squares, diagonals, receding blocks, terra cotta, twilight colours,
tiled, oblong shapes, Chagall, all tangled to
the London River (beyond, the Essex marshes). No ships tonight.

You know how it is in a dream when the sky is vast
but intimate things are closer? I could see
and smell and taste and feel on my ankles
and legs, the turbulent black water (diesel, oil and tar), the

currents moving, stronger
than alcohol or memory or muscle, the white froth
crashed up, waves spume crying
under the pier by the pilot station —

all from the floor of my bedroom, looking through
that window, as the waters broke
on the shingle and the stones
knocked into each other, again, against, again —

and the black, black sky suddenly lit up
like fireworks, nuclear night: red, yellow, white upon white
trails of stars in flaring forms
blossom-bursts of light, later than midnight, incandescence —

bursting and failing and fading and bursting
and blazing and trailing, all through the frame
of my childhood's bedroom window, my feet on the carpeted floor:
No dream tonight, no softness in the memory. This, the burning deck.

3

Clearances

It is time to stop writing about the Highland Clearances etc.
Iain Crichton Smith

Kilmartin Glen

I never saw the intricate connections
with quite this sunny clarity before,
such intimate revealing of relations
in brilliance, and at such an hour:
the West and Islands open to the sea
and Ireland, always seemed to be
alive with colour: bright blue waters,
emeralds and snow; but shapes and movement,
glacial striations, ox-bow lakes, tidal rivers,
hill-tops making patterns to each other —
all connect in vision as the art of men
and women finds its laws in natural
reciprocation: raindrops in a quiet pool
form expanding spirals on the bending plane:
an ancient brooch, the lanulae —
silver, gold: water, sunlight, eyes
to see the clearness of design. And this
takes place in mind, imagination:
across 10,000 years, while now
outside the car my father drives, the rain
drives down on grass and bracken, heather
rocks and hills and lochs and lochans,
midges and elusive little fish. The forestry
have camouflaged the earth's wet dark
antiquity; the road between Kilmartin
and the ferry just approaching Oban is
impatient, twisty, a hard fast exit through
this valley of old ghosts. And yet the vision stays
perception, the clarity of sunlight's
careful disposition, in
this undifferentiated time.

The Rivers of Space
for Wilson Harris

Why do we turn ourselves away, like this, from sunlight into
dark, divining rock? The fissures in the mountains take us, allow us
into themselves, but there is no easy air, meandering
in dances like a greensward pastoral, or turning corners
broadly and in leisure, as a man might walk in
Jonson's Penshurst. Not for these and not for us: a
thrawnness insists upon acceptance of a range that can't
be chosen easily.

— A haggard face with hollow eyes,
an arm set leaning, firmly, on a fence: and in behind, a field, a cottage,
comfort — a wife and child, the give and take,
dogs and teapots, china, cutlery, pleasantries that keep
alive and cover up the sheer urge of meaning leaning within. No
comfort in that, except in turning from it, and often little grace,
back to that home, that hearth. And then to find that urgency
alive as well in others, men and women, wife and child,
flashing in an adamantine glance,
so rare it is, so common.

— You're smiling as we look at the child, and he is
smiling back at you. You comment on the wisdom in
the smile; it seems to come from a distant place in time.
I'm thinking of my father and his father's name that stretches back.
The hardest thing of all is to say what it means as simply and
as clearly as it can be said, and it's simply that we know
it can't be said at all in any other way. And that's
why we turn ourselves away, like this, from easy
dancing afternoons, from sunlight, into cavernous divining rock:
whole theatres of sound with rivers and with music, running and
cascading in them: falling through air, the rivers of space.

A Proper Respect for Horses
(after Vladimir Mayakovsky)

Horse-hoofs clattered
clatter-clunk!   clatter-clunk!
Clunk!
clatter-clunk!
clatter-clunk!

Wind shoved
and the slippery ice
on its shoes, in the street —
in a trice, in a beat,
in a skid
its legs went out from under it.
Crump!

And all at once
the mocking crowd
appeared and with their big mouths gawping,
all gaw-haw, hee-haw, haa haa
surrounded it
in their fancy flared jeans, all the fashion just then.
'The poor old horse is slipped!'
'The tired old horse is down!' they sneered.
And all along Kuznetsky, they howled at it and laughed.

All
Except for me.
I didn't join that crowd to laugh at her.
I went right up and looked
into that chestnut eye —

the street tipped over like
a glass off a table —

while I knelt there to see
the tear-drops scramble down the cheek and neck
and slip into her mane, and hide

And some strange sort of common sense
spilled out of my heart and flowed
running like a waterfall, suddenly undammed.

'Oh horse,
don't cry!
Listen to me now.
Don't think that they're any better than you.
Oh, child, don't you know, horses are we all,
to be honest,
in the end: everyone's a horse
in some kind of way.'

Ah well. Maybe she was old and wise
and didn't need my words.
Or maybe I was just too soft.

But there and then
the horse
jerks up
clatters to her feet —
whinnies in the frosty air
and gallops down the street!
My chestnut child!
With a flick of her tail
like a yearling
she canters into her stall
ready for work once again
for the life that's worth it all!

Edinburgh, High Street: Nocturne

A forest of a hundred thousand dæmons —
D.O. Fagunwa's African head held undergrowths
and tunnels that my present occupation is
to notice and to indicate, right here, mediævally moving
in the castellated cobbled and diagonal
of sloping street suffused below the yellowish
diffusing streetlamp there that's just beside my
bedroom window. The snow was fully occupied
around the corner of the building and I walked
from living room to hall to kitchen back to hall
to bedroom, looking out examining the tiny flakes
that made another atmosphere, beyond the
double glazing: the dark is filled with white flecks, but not
quite fully occupied itself, while all the spirits of the place
are on the mile and moving, in subterranean ways
and wynds, below the mile. 'You have a whole theatre here.'
The oblong lights in residential flats in buildings
stories high will all go out at last and all
those occupants will go beneath the earth.
The tourists walk below and take the guided walks and know
there is a question mark that cannot be subtracted
from their answers, whispered: where? what more?
what lies beneath? A drunken soldier swore he'd found
a tunnel in the dungeons of the castle at the height,
which led him to a maze of unmapped arteries beneath,
that he emerged at Holyrood, under some confusion.
An evening might leave you like that, but the groan
of buses and cars and taxis, sirens at midnight, 2
and 3 am; road-menders widening the pavements and
re-cobbling: the grumbling sounds of day and night
seep into the stones and the cold volcanic earth beneath.
Apocrypha and atmosphere. Kitsch and tartan plastic dolls.
Voodoo kilted effigies and bagpipes playing all the time,
somewhere nearby just out of sight of hearing —
A sloping world where all secure dualities (Argyll/Montrose)
are partnered in an incomplete notation, a sinking,
structuredly preserved configuration, and as the stars

look down, a brittle, bright, tough-souled and dark
and dangerous, and friendly, night-time constellation.

Cities on the Plain
(Prelude to 'Insomnia 3')

The cities are mazed on an endless plain:
Edinburgh, Paris: dream of them with causeways, bridges:
Notre Dame arising from the Seine, Edinburgh Castle
beside the Eiffel Tower. Jumble them up and
sharp slopes rise. Clefts and valleys fall.
The shadows of the Royal Mile are
warped between translucent screens: the sun sheets through
the Centre Pompidou. Add Istanbul, the now and then,
and Glasgow. Open ferries navigate
the broad ship-crowded Bospheros and Clyde,
beside the sharply spired Cathedral
sheltered in the shadow of Victorian Necropolis, as around
the hill a labyrinth of graves
passes the Blue Mosque,
into the netted streets that lead
to the covered bazaar: gold, brass, bronze,
the arteries of coin and trade,
glasses and tasses of tea, silver
spoons glitter and carpets roll and unroll in
rich fringed patterned reds; beneath even this,
the cisterns, a network of platforms by Roman canals,
leading off to chartered tunnels, white arches by the walled-up pillars, gloom,
for beneath even this, a deeper plan, another set of tunnels
spreads its arms out who knows where?
Now out into air once again. You realize,
the streets are all deserted. It's early dusk. Find the Finnieston Crane
and climb the iron ladder to the highest point of the cabin's roof,
let's smoke a cigarette and look: the cities all mesh into one another.
You can see them stretched out on the plain:
Rome, New York...and Hong Kong, Singapore:
the ruins of the Parthenon, Liberty's rising arm and torch,
the high rise heat conglomerates, sluggish streams slide sampans,
scows, Brooklyn Bridge leads into Sago Lane.
The cities are endless on the endless plain. Now, at last,
come down once again to the street. Night falls. We'll walk.

Insomnia 3
(after Marina Tsvetayeva)

My city is enormous. All cities run together. It's night. I rise.
My home is full of sleeping souls. I go out in the night.
Am I a son or father? Husband? Wife, or mother? Daughter too?
Bereaved perhaps, somehow. What's in my mind the most?
Only the presence of cities, and of night.

The wind sweeps out a way for me: leaves and paper, newsprint from
a century of yesterdays, blows up in spirals, gutters, sags,
and music faintly, ghostly, in the keen violin-stringed air
from somewhere, winding through each street, tonight, till dawn, as if
twined through the rib-cage of my skeleton breast, and on.

Tall trees, black buildings, windows full of light
and music falling thinly from the heights to land
like flowers in my hands, as I'm walking. I open them,
and look around and back at where
my footsteps were. It is as if the sound they made continued, by me,
following, but nobody's looking at my moving shadow. Nobody's
there and nothing of me now remains here.

The lights are threaded beads of gold, in every building
round my eyes; my throat breathes in
the empty night. My mouth tastes city leaves. (A fox appears in shadows
by the trees, and hesitates, and then retreats.) I walk alone
for freedom from the bondage of each day.
Oh friends who read this, now, imagine me.
See me as I am, inhabiting the streets, walking through the nights
as they touch each endless city on the vast plains of this world.
I only am your ghost, a voice. I only am your dream, no more.

Nostalgia

O Alter Duft aus Märchenzeit
('Old fragrance from Once Upon a Time')
— Schoenberg, last song from *Pierrot Lunaire*

Woodsmoke catch,
      a small fire,
the nostrils and the right side of the throat
      the horses in the lower field
white turnips from the earth beneath the little den of trees
a circle of stones
      to be sitting on
the bitter tang and taste, the sharp smell
crunch of white turnip
      between teeth
      on the tongue, saliva working
      in the throat —
a higher field of corn, higher than the boys
running into hide-and-seek
      escaping from the cornstalks, onto the verandah
      of the big shed, squeezing through the gap
      between the door and the stacked wood
      climbing over the planks, in the scent of wood, up
      hiding
            then, when discovery approached, out!
      climbing to the skylight, out onto the roof
      sliding down, then off
in an amazing trajectory, through the air, out
onto the sapling trunk of a silver birch a yard away, heedless,
sliding down it like a pole
ripping the slender branches, the cruelty of children, the pursuer above you,
following, the tree asway in sunlight and excitement,
racing for the base camp, the kennel, now: feet on the ground and running
      the kennel where we set
      a railway sleeper on
      the roof, to see-
      saw up into higher air, almost
      above the big shed

     Look! You can see!
  beyond the trees, above them as the field slopes down,
     over the fields, the silver canal,
    wound like the slough of a snake,
  past farms and clouds and houses —
All the way to Africa!

New Zealand Pastoral

The sun has turned the tidal bay and hills beyond it silver,
all a single silver hue, the sand beyond the mussel-beds
is streaked and slipping, silver strands of light.
The sparrows dipping, swooping from the saffron rice leftover
on the board, on the deck, down
                      then up-in-under
the branches of pohutukawa trees,
                  give glints of
similar silver, sudden flecks.

Outside, the silence is perfect, perfectly accented by
the distances of sound: relative scales of birdsong, the
deep-throb intermittent bell-bird's call; then the occasional
car, a slow rise and swish on the low road there,
and what our voices would be, were we talking, laughing, bright-
eyed, on a stroll across the tidal sands, walking into distance.

           It looks as though the silver foil
you used to find in cigarette packs, or the baking foil
you use to wrap a roast in, were cut in long thin strips and
laid out slightly wrinkled and refracting, over a dark serrated strip
of forested promontory, and the clouds coming down, the
sunlight whitening through them, turn the further mountain range
to silver-grey.

        So much for the baking foil,
our present world outside: the roast is here inside,
the four of us, lit up, the rising pile of Guinness cans, the
rugby football match, half done on that TV.

Clearances
for James

The clouds go over
singly, or in fleets, trailing
raggedly back, against a sky
where looming vaults of rain
come over too. Then the sky lets loose:
the shades of grey become uncountable,
the rain comes down on everything, diagonal, banks:
the windows, roof, the wooden deck,
the trees around, the green slopes run
with mud, the fields below are soaked and fill;
the road becomes a grey and moving river.

The baby hasn't heard this sound before: the heavy rain
on the iron roof, and cries himself
to sleep, at last, as the downpour
eases off. It must be time to leave.
The weather is an actual farewell.

I used to think the old Gaels of Ireland,
or the west of Scotland, knew
so little of our modern world.
It seemed they were a pastoral people
and burdened with a culture of conservatism.
But clearances are always strong in the mind,
the images recurrent, the rubble of the ruined homes,
the ghosts of children, animals, and men
and women helpless in the face of the event.

Farewells and birth, there are some things
no clues or forms of knowledge alter
in themselves. I won't say they can't help.
They knew about departure, those old people,
and the kinds of life we deal with here
require that inherited wisdom. Now
the heavy showers have passed, but different shades of grey
reflect, refract unnumbered tones of light.

It's time to pack what we have and can carry.
It's time to take what we can, and go. The boy
will not remember this, the landscape
of his parents, unless we do.

        (Coromandel, 25/9/94)

Kylesku

All afternoon the sun burned your forehead and face,
driving for miles through peatscrapes,
bare rock ridges rising from moorland, driving through rain,
mist trailed past, the sunlight strong from the blue
where the clouds were broken.

We were the last to go through, after
the bath or shower, the tables were pretty in heavy pink covers.
Outside the windows the jetty slips down to the loch,
and the boat pulls up past the seals,
heads bobbing, water lapping the boat, leaning towards moorings.

Blues come up out of the water, as darker blurs blend
on the hills; the water is exactly H2O and moves
in particular shapes all the time. The air smells of peat. I'm glad
you're here, and know it's that
the other way around, as well.

It wouldn't be if there was any
other way but this. The sea is hushed at dusk,
and in the gloamin when I'll walk beside you, with you, up
the sloping street with houses on the one side only,
to where the sign this afternoon read 'Post

Office': your picture-cards all stamped and ready,
written in your hand. I'll strain to hear
nothing, clearly there, but welcome, quiet,
welcome, and, keep moving, from
the landscape all around us.

Going Away Poem
for Chris Larsen

the river takes its little tributary
in and runs away downstream
the trees create green cool, and
click: a photograph, two
men with their suggestions of
two smiles. It is as if the air has
suddenly cleared of smoke. Old soldiers
in the big house up the hill recuperate, they
fade back into colours, original tints,
bullet holes are mended in a sequence of unendingly
precise late afternoons. It is the one fine day
of summer. The laughter of my playful sons
is playing in my mind, a world away.

Chris, you and I remember good and bad
times, colours, fevers of belief and hesitations,
and mistakes.
                    Let this stand for other things.

Paint

Objects do not exist for me except in so far as a harmonious relationship exists between them and also between them and myself. When one attains this harmony one reaches a sort of intellectual non-existence which makes everything possible and right.
— Georges Braque

How do you do that?
A few broad brush-strokes:
Still life with top hat
Or red on white is Strawberries,
Fresh. I was standing in New York
and thinking of my Uncle John
looking at the Paley collection
in the Museum of Modern Art.
You get the impression that the man
enjoyed his paintings.
He had an eye for nudes.
My Uncle John
was the first in the family
to acquire a freezer.
When I visited once,
he showed it to me proudly.
It was white, horizontal,
and very big. When
he opened it, the only
things inside it,
lying at the bottom,
brilliantly coloured
were 2 cock pheasants,
totally stiff. He reached his
right arm in
and lugged them out.
I suggested 'Dinner?' but
he frowned and
shook his head
'These are for painting.'

Still life with pheasants.
Of course.

Cézanne
(At the Tate Gallery, London, February 1996)

It is the blatant evidence of the brush
that shows us the subtlety of the relations of colour
in landscape, in still life, in the forms of being
human and the shapes of relationship between
apples and oranges and jugs and tablecloths, between
people, and between the eye of the male
artist and the bodies of different women;
it is this coincidence of revelation
in texture and in tone (in brush stroke and in colour)
that opens the gaze of the viewer
who watches each painting closely
again then anew then afresh
to the act of visual and therefore imaginative
construction of the world, taking place
at the moment, moment by moment.
The construction is selective (taking place
in the moment), certainly; but it is constructive
of certainty: the mind, through the eye, to reality
the real, through the painting (the act, painting) to
the creating mind. This empowers, just as it
makes vulnerable. Thus it provides a moral,
as well as an aesthetic, imperative,
and a political context for it
by demonstrating the processes of its own creation,
and the watcher on the threshold crosses the threshold,
every time.

Passacaglia
for Ronald Stevenson

*The movement of a passacaglia is the movement of water
flowing in a broad stream, underneath the ice upon a border river.*

1
The miles of peat-bog, tufts of cotton and the rain pelting across
the flat expanse of moor, my friends and I, our jackets collared up,
marched over, with spring-stepped stride and wide determination,
intentional, heading for the steeple edge and end of land
near Elgol, facing the sea. Soaked, our coats still warmed
us as we sclimmed and clambered down the cliff-cut
edges of rock, and through the fissured caverns to the open ledge
of stone that faced the sea front: the weight of the Atlantic breaking —
water smashes stone and ledge — drenched, clinging
to the wall of rock as the sea heaves monumental tides
of dreck-free ocean, threatening brutality and equal in its opposition
to rock, and in its natural indifference to creatures live beside it.

2
There is another place where broken ice-floes heave upon the weight
of the Atlantic under them, and the mass of waves is something else —
hard on the edge of sea and land, the rock dropping down, our
puny human selves beside it, only fighting momentarily —

3
But these are coasts and cuts —
rock and ocean, massive oppositions.

Think of a river in the borders, a
broad and curving stream, its
natural beauty covered with another,
closed over by ice, and the trees not bare
and skeletal, but crusted with the crystal salt
and diamond of winter's world.

                And know our music
moves beneath, a movement going on, under
the pressure of that carapace,
running —
to all the trouble there is
to come when it reaches the sea.

Sankey Hymns

What did they know of reverence,
the sailors' congregation? In Stornoway
they gathered, an hour before
the regular service
began, and filled the wooden pews and raised
their voices in mass praise. Resolve
of hardihood was theirs. Let reverence be left
to those more pious worshippers
who occupied the space left vacant when these men
went down to the sea to their ships, once again.
It's not a skill that's needed, catching fish.
Accuracy, yes. And Strength. A physical fact so prevalent
the eyes and voices of these men reveal it
every moment. Thinking was too slow for them,
reverence unhelpful.
                    Let them stand in Stornoway,
and sing for God to help them live and work.

MacDiarmid on Whalsay

1.   *A Glass of Cold Water, Mid-Afternoon*

Some like it hot, after dinner, but poets know their
preference: A house at home in Arctic winds in
the outbreak of war, the North Sea when it was
the German, spike-helmetted, silver and black,
glittering (ever the best in uniform, the Nazi sky
and ocean, inhumanly and humanly unmerciful). And
you're there trying hard, doing what you can to help
the listed poems escape. Weather is one thing,
daily, accumulating change. This is another: this
is the climate. Set yourself against it: the words
lean on the window-panes and rattle their frames
like iron bars; night and the stormtroops lean in.

2.   *Air Salt Stone*

Benign on the inlets and islets of inside, of
Langerhans, the warm sun shines for a long time
each and every day, on all the 'corrugations' and
the 'coigns'. Each word is a delicate finger-tip's
print tracing gently with pressure on each turning
shape, the stones themselves mere metaphors for
these attempts to charge them with a meaning.
Night earns it, but, day brings it, sometimes. Not
every day. All every day will bring is, mushrooms,
mackerel, washing-up, good water from the well.
But some days like that sunshine, touching, lat-
erally, over all: inside, out, and there, benign.

3.   *Valda and Michael*

I see her hands and arms, the strengths in bone
and muscle, her fingers round the string run
through the gills of sillocks, her clothes coarse

and warm, her independence, guidance, giving,
glee. Her laughter, lips, her voice. His voice.
His march of childhood, sheer Shetlandic
balance, care, assertiveness, set in a world
where shelter is less frequent and more welcome,
the edge never easy but ubiquitous, the crash and
cry of gulls' flight, waves, time marked, ferries
booming horns away, bells ringing into all the
horizons opening out and closing in to deadlines.

The Jungle Books
for Edwin Morgan at 80

Dear Eddie,
     I wish you continuity and love, and since what is to come comes on
so many different valencies, remember what has been works that way too.

The garden of the room at 4 o'clock. Details: a brazen Chinese dragon on
                                               the hearth,
a chintzy coffee table-top, an ash tray, box of matches, Russian wooden
                                               cigarette-box,
books. An underwater atmosphere of watchfulness and silence, as if
                                               that old rock
python Kaa were snoozing, one eye open, just nearby. *Your words have*
                                             been heard.

While Norman's smoking endlessly with Caliban, you're
flying through the dark frost-scented air, Ariel-free over pines and lochs
                                               and sleeping
like our 5-year-old, away before Adam, 'curled up in a nest of twigs and
                                             boughs'
dropping himself on the Persian rug, on his clasped hands on a pillow,
                                           under a
blanket, like that, into another world that takes him back, a self-
                                           determined astronaut,
to Scotland's Arabian nights. What happens when Bach hears the sound
                                           of the sea?

Remember those trees, last and first men, first raising an arm and a hand
                                           to a branch,
the atavism, swinging into languages like Tarzan, lonely in adventures
                                           and coincidences
multiplied; meeting the creatures in all their strange colours and sizes;
populations, frontiers; gliding low and fast across those miles and miles
                                           and miles of old Barsoom,
like fen around Cam. Take off from bridges! Fly!
                        That drumlin runway called Great Western Road!
An endless flight and a fine resolve, like Carson on Venus, lost in the
                                           forests of Amtor,

or like MacKenna's gold, knowing the map to miracles and earthquakes,
'There is no map,' MacKenna said. But there was. There is. It happens.
These things good men believe in, affinities of mind and mortal memory.
Or the man with the harmonica ('He not only plays, he can shoot too...')
Or Doughty come back from the desert and dawn. Yol. That's the way.
Or riding like the rain-god Shalako, for eight days in the summer
of 1882, hearing no sound but the hooves of the horse,
the creak of the saddle, the wind in the mountains and
dusty dry arroyos. Or undersea with Nemo and Ned Land, that
thick-calved harpooner, Nautilian in battle: to overthrow the righteous,
                                            not the damned!
If it's Blake or the Establishment, I'll side with you.
As London said, Go on, be scared, we mean to do it all! *Hwæt!*

Riffled childhood reading, and when I skim back I can see —
you were there already, in seas and cities, deserts, Cathkin Braes
                                    and Strathaven,
old and new, in Lanarkshire, in Glasgow and in words, leaving no
                                    trace but everywhere
encouragement. Now I know, you're 80 and I'm half that, but
as old J.B.Y. to young J.B.Y., 'If you want to do anything really
                                    worth while, some
part of you must never, ever, ever grow up.'

— All charts of the lunar seas,
All maps of the stellar oceans, Stravinsky's
King of the Stars is singing for you.

The Symphony of a Thousand

The heart of any city is the labyrinth.
For me it was the Concert Hall on Saturday,
The 13th of October 1990: Mahler 8.
It looks like Berlin, the Brandenburg Gate:
beyond these spartan columns is
a different economy. Edward, Chris, myself.
We'd noted it three months before.
We'd set our minds and hearts on it
but left the thing too late. Yet not too late: it came to this.
That day, the night itself: 7:15.
The queue winds in at last: sold out. No chance.
Split up! Edward joins the little group forlornly waiting for returns;
I set out round the building, looking for touts;
Chris goes off on his own, into the building, to see.
We reconvene five minutes later: nothing.
No tickets returned, no cancelled seats, the happy crowds.
The strong lights in the foyer accentuate it all.
The time is 7:20. Try again.
We meet again at 7:25. Nothing. The bell rings out. Ed begins to show
his resignation. Chris suddenly appears, out of the crowd,
a faint smile on his face: 'I think
I may have found a way.'
             He leads us through the chattering suits,
the champagne, chilled white wines, fruit juice.
The crowd thins out. The voices dwindle. Silence.
A bright, broad, empty stairwell takes us up, around, and higher to
a panelled corridor. The doors are polished wood,
as are the walls, and almost imperceptible. Chris leans on one.
It opens. And we enter a shadowy, high-ceilinged room, purple-
curtained, where three long tables are covered and spread
for a banquet: the gleaming silver cutlery, polished plate,
bottles of wine, carafes of water, flowers. Nobody's here
but us. Post-concert celebration, planned. The bell is ringing
once again, but distantly. Chris takes us round the tables to
another door, an anteroom, another stairwell, higher now, it's 7:28, and up
and round and there: the last of them, the audience,
are going through the concert auditorium's swing doors.

And we walk forward, not to be denied.
But still polite. Two sentences correctly pitched
deliver our state to the usher: I give to him our strong desire to see.
No tickets, but. And then that pale young man's pure Glasgow: 'Ach,
well,' he glances in. 'Ye've come this far. Just slip round there.'
— The empty row above the children's chorus,
The balcony, stage left, up high. The timing is exact.
It's 7:31 and God, precisely then, what sounds begin,
                                         what Christ descends!

It's twenty to eleven. The three of us
are sitting in the Third Eye Centre, coffee
on the table, there. Silent still, ears full of it.
And Chris unbuttons his coat half-guiltily and opens it
yet still with a firm half-smile and in one movement
lifts and sets in front of us a shadowy bottle of red.

The Viaduct, Millheugh

There is no higher iron bridge in Scotland
this viaduct of spars and beams and rivets
the forest rises thick on either side
the river runs from white falls to a broad brown stream below
rare birds can be seen there

Once some thought of dynamite
— children might have fallen, anyway it's ugly;
       now it is preserved by order
Trains have long ago abandoned it
and grass grows on the pebbles by the sleepers
but it's strong and stands untrembling
high in the clear winter air
       an undistracted image of attachment
bank to bank and wood to wood

       I've crossed it slowly, back and forth
so many times —
       unfrequented, still assured
there is a way
       so high

4

The Long Reach

*Man is only part of a splendour,
and a memory of it.*
Jack B. Yeats

To My Brother
(after César Vallejo)

Brother, I miss you.
(If only our father
were not so far away,
perhaps I would never have looked
for brothers in the landscape.)

But today the sun is shining
        on this stone bench
it's warm, white, mottled,
        but hard as a wooden pew
and I'm sitting here in the warmth
        and missing you.

When we were boys, Nana would call down
        from the house, high up on the slope.
Her voice would tell us not to fight, come back —
        but you were different, always fought —
        we never did see eye-to-eye.

But I miss you all the same.
How much time we wasted fighting.
All I want just now is for
        you to be beside me, here,
brother.
            If I go and hide,
play hide-and-seek,
        you won't catch me, I know.
And now, I know, I never can catch you.

You hid yourself one August night for ever
And now I feel like sadness is my life.

Oh, listen, will you, hear this,
hear this if you can: come back, come
out of hiding, here, tonight. Nana's getting worried.

Trilce 61
(after César Vallejo)

When the red sun is balanced on the rim of the horizon
I dismount
        in front of the
verandah, in front
of the closed door
and the shuttered windows
of the house I set out from at dawn. Nobody's here.

There's the stone bench
where Nana bore my brother.
He saddled the horses I rode bareback
down avenues, by trellised garden walls,
a village boy,
        the bench I left for daily yellow sunlight
to soak the pain of childhood,
but pain soaks back and permeates
this page.

The horse is a lonely god in a different world
its sneeze is a lonely call in another language
its long neck bends, it noses in the dust on the verandah
        its ears flick up, it
hesitates, its thick neck comes back up, frightened, alert.
It's seeing spirits.

Papa must be up, grumbling, telling himself I've been out late,
And my sisters getting the next meal ready, humming as they work.
We want for almost nothing, but an egg
is in my heart somehow, obstructing.

We were a family not long ago
but nobody is watching any longer.
There are no lights in windows now to wait us.

I call again. Nothing.

Tears are close. Horse snorts again.
They're all asleep, forever now.
So soundly that the horse begins to nod,
gently, slowly, as if it were reflected in the rearview of a car
driving away in a dust-cloud,
nodding by the faces of my family, turning to look out once more
through the back window,
pale in the light of farewell,
      nodding, that it's all
all right,
      and you can
go to sleep now

everything's okay

Lullaby

*Dreams are secret diplomacy
between states that you'll never know existed —*

I would like you now
to fall asleep, imagining
those moments where the pulse
takes over gently,
slowly, the rhythm of
your blood, and circulation clasps
your hands you're warm now, sleeping
gently, as you are —
As you are going to sleep now,
be dreaming of someone —
let it be someone
who does not lie beside you, but
who lives nearby you, loves you, let it be
a dreaming of
a notion of
        that nearness, fondly —
now and like that, you might fall
into sleep, smiling, alone.

Kissing in Cars

A simple recognition of mistakes,
of roads we'd been on, never
should have taken,
maybe. But maybe it's as well this way.
The way it's worked out took a funny pattern or
a network of uncertainties, a strange
uncertain sequence of events, by roads,
leading us to this, together in
                        a parked car in Nevada
your lips touching mine, and just
this daft pleasure: kissing in cars.

The Long Reach

On the green plains of Kent, on the Canterbury Road,
under the highest arches of sky and the big silver banners of cloud,
where the long low marshes of the river's south bank are north-west,
marked by parishes, churches, graveyards, where Pip's young siblings'
lozenges lie in rustling leaves at Cooling and every headstone's silence hides
a Magwitch, where, to the north, Whitstable skims on its mudflat
out into the estuary, birdsong and memories of 1960s murders
(a harder kind of violence than any we see much of here today), where,
south-east, the sheer vanilla stone of the Cathedral and an older
martyrdom, navigate the crowds in their small city, and where, all round
the Cinque Ports, and Margate, Ramsgate, Deal, Dover, Folkestone,
the pilot boats go out and come back in, and the pilots look back
on the grazing sheep on Romney Marsh near the great almost luminous ball
of the power station at Dungeness, and the two trees on the curvature
together make a rearing horse, while here, on the green curved plains of
                                                                                 Kent,
we park the car beside the pilgrims' road by a long low pub and stand
beside it looking all around, from Rochester downriver to the crumbling
                                                                                      cliffs
in the south, from one bleak house to another, from over into France
back up the run of the Channel, along upriver to London, and
turn and look up once again, reading the name
on the tiled roof there, and then lock the car, and go in.

Of Love

There's an old film called The Minister's Wife *where Cary Grant plays an angel come to earth to work a few miracles. One shot reveals him, hands clasped behind his back, his back to a table with an almost empty bottle of wine on it. Another drink is called for. Unobserved, his index finger points to the low meniscus, runs up the side of the bottle, and the content refills, by magic. Love works unobtrusively, like that.*

If I could bring them all together,
what would I have?

An image of her, smiling in excitement,
approaching in the crowd on London Bridge.

An image of her, thoughtful in her yellow dress,
walking down the grey slope of the street.

And an image of her, at nightfall, hand in hand with me,
crossing the field to a tryst, with kindling fire inside.

And of her, under the tree, laughter light as a bird's wings,
her face, her hands strong as branches.

And of her, standing in the doorway bidding me goodbye.
And of her again, standing in the doorway, returned at last forever.

If I put them all together now, in twenty-seven years,
and called to the ends of the earth, all exultations, fears,

and no predictions count, yet I would say
with certainty: There was love. Now, let it stay.

The Transit of Venus

Geometry of contact
                as 6 hrs past
made compasses from one point to
another,
        an angle therefore figured indicates
the only world
              particular endurance and the will
allows to make love happen in,
           by virtue of the calculated distances
the means it takes forever to devise
lifetimes of devotion, against the measureless tides

        : like the clock at Beauvais
a mechanism made to signal, chimes each hundred years:
a sound its maker could hear only once. And that's
like love, or children, all
           that mortal being matters.
The Transit of Venus:
     The way love moves
              the orbits of the sun and other stars.

Late Afternoon

You will grow old. Your reflection in the sliding doors
will vanish in the glass more quickly, but
your shadow on the landscape on the green
hills far away will stay for longer now, like this.